Six Questions
for
Leading Achievers

Clive Hook

Thoughts, tips, techniques, reflections and worksheets for
your leadership journey

Copyright © 2016 Clive Hook

ISBN: 978-1-326-86771-3

Leadership and Action Learning

In our company ClearWorth, we put action learning at the heart of our approach to personal and professional development. There are two fundamental aspects of action learning that influence how we design, develop and deliver learning.

The first is that real learning happens in real life – not in the classroom, not while reading a book, looking at a case study or watching a PowerPoint. Real-life learning happens when you say or do something and get some feedback. By "feedback" I don't necessarily mean somebody giving you a report on your performance - although that is one form. Feedback is you getting information about the results or outcome of what you just said or did. There are only three options. Things get better, stay the same or get worse. Each of these options has the potential for learning if you're open to it.

The second aspect is that learning doesn't happen unless there is a question that needs to be answered or addressed. Note the difference – there may not be an answer but the question is worth examination and consideration. Like Reg Revans – the founding father of action learning – I think questions are more important than answers.

The problem with answers is that they may not actually be answers at all because they were formed at a different time, in a different place with different circumstances. That's why we don't use case studies. They're written about something that happened in a unique set of circumstances at some time in the past.

The problem in the case study may or may not have been solved – they usually are solved because it makes a more satisfying case to read. But the answer only suited that particular situation. What IBM or Apple or 3M or whoever did at a given time is interesting reading – but trying to cut and paste the lessons into today's volatile economic circumstances is madness.

The wonderful thing about good questions is that they encourage thinking, intelligent conversations, creativity, experimentation and innovation. Maintaining a spirit of curiosity is, I believe, the healthiest outlook for a human being.

When you think you know it all then life must surely be boring – or you're too arrogant to notice.

In developing our approach to personal and professional development for people in positions of leadership (I'm avoiding the word "leader" at the moment for a good reason) we have stayed true to our learning philosophy and have built it around questions, not bunches of pre-prepared answers or simple formulae.

I will, of course, cite some ways of thinking about a specific topic, but I hope it will always be in the spirit of a proposal or suggestion or prompt for thinking, rather than a definitive answer.

I suppose the other thing that we've learned from Reg and his approach to learning is the difference between a puzzle and a problem. He sadly died before Sudoku was all the rage – it would have provided him with a perfect example of the difference as an illustration of where action learning is most appropriate.

Sudoku is a puzzle – in the end there is an answer and you know when you've got it because the numbers 1 to 9 are in the right places in the right rows and columns. It might be hard, but you know when you've finished – and experience will help you learn how to spot your mistakes earlier and probably get better at it as you go.

A problem is different. There isn't a pre-defined answer and, both while you're working on it and when you think you've finished, you don't know if that's the solution or not.

Our world in ClearWorth is the world of working with people: and people problems are the perfect examples. One solution does not fit all and even when you think you know what the answer is, you can find you're completely wrong.

There's nearly always another aspect or layer or piece that you weren't told or didn't understand or even realise existed. Fascinating and frustrating at the same time. It's what makes life interesting and what keeps us in business at ClearWorth.

So, what follows is an introduction to thinking about you and your role in leadership. You may or may not have a job title that includes or infers the word "leader". You may not even describe yourself as having a job.

What I think you want to do is to have an effect and influence on people and I hope it's with their best interests at heart. You want them to do better, have more, be happier, be more contented, achieve their potential, have less worries or whatever it is.

I believe leadership is about being of service to others. You can still do that and be in charge, of course. If you host a party, then it's your party – you're in charge, but your intention is that people enjoy themselves and have a good time.

You are offering your hospitality, your food, wine, home, company, music and warmth. You probably have some boundaries and rules in mind because it's your stuff and you expect them to play within those rules – don't break or steal stuff for example. But still you are in service to them. That's very like leadership to me.

This book and the approach is designed to make you think about you, your role and the people you serve. I believe the rules apply whether you're thinking about your company, team, department, family, community, association, club or project.

Now when I say "rules" I mean principles, not sets of "must-do" or "how-to" instructions because (as we said earlier) there are no nice neat answers.

The difference between average people and achieving people is their perception of and response to failure

John C. Maxwell

The motto of our Leading Achievers' Club is:

ARS DUCENDI ARS DISCENDI EST

– the art of leading is the art of learning. I hope your life is filled with questioning, thinking and learning.

What or Who are Leading Achievers?

Is that people who are leaders in their field of achieving or is that people who lead others who achieve? Good question. The answer is "yes". My experience is that the very best leaders not only achieve tremendous results but help create the opportunity and environment for others to achieve and get more of what they want.

So, whether you see yourself as the achiever or the leader of others' achievements, these questions are for you. I characterise them as the questions you should have the answers to - so that if you were asked by a TV interviewer, you could look straight at the camera and answer them without hesitation.

When I help leaders prepare for being in the public arena, I call this "practised spontaneity". Some of the high-profile leaders I've worked with must know the questions they could be asked at any moment.

They need to have thought through what their considered answer is – it's that or face the prospect of looking an idiot.

In recent times, we've all seen examples of those in the media. Those who have been publicly disgraced or just left looking foolish and inadequate.

In summary, then, the six questions are:

1 Who do you think you are? – What do you know or not know about you, and how much is in the public domain? And there are two extra words to add to the question which make all the difference.

2 What do you stand for? – We've all got values and points of view and we tend to think we're right. Some of those values significantly affect the way we think, feel and behave. So how do your values show themselves in the way you approach life and leadership?

3 Why should they follow you? – If you are to be of service then people will have free choice about whether they come to your party or follow your path. What is it that defines a leader? The answer's a surprise to many people.

4 What will be different? – Leadership is about change.. One of my mentors described it to me as "A leader takes you somewhere you haven't been before". So, do you know where that place is and can you explain it?

5 Who's on your side? – Political intelligence - its very name conjures up Machiavellian scheming and plotting. It's much more benign – but a vital skill if you're going to get people to buy in to your idea.

6 Who listens when you speak? – If the message is important then you want to increase the chances of it being heard, understood and accepted. Without an engaged audience, you're a voice crying in the wilderness.

Unless we base our sense of identity upon the truth of who we are, it is impossible to attain true happiness.

Brenda Shoshanna

Question One

Who Do You Think You Are?

Joe and Harry are two of my heroes. They developed something that has both made me money and given people wonderful insights for more than 60 years. The Johari window developed by Joseph Luft and Harrington Ingham in 1955 is a heuristic – a thing designed to start conversations and thinking. The topic of this conversation is you and what's known or not known about you. It's been developed in various ways over the years. The original version gave you a list of 57 adjectives to choose from. We have a version of that but I tend to prefer people to just do some thinking about the relative size of each of their window panes and what would best describe them in those panes.

So, our version of their original model is

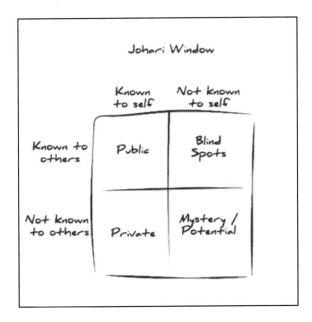

Public – This is "stuff" (a favourite technical term of mine) that you know about yourself and people know about you, too. Your general appearance, your skin and hair colour, your style of clothing, some of your thoughts and views, perhaps some of the acknowledged adjectives about how you are in the public domain. This is the "you" we all know.

Blind Spots – That awful moment when you hear your recorded voice when singing or see yourself on video and can't believe you sound or look like that. It's quite different to how you thought you were. As a singer, I have had to accept that what I think I sound like is not what I actually sound like. The noise that my head hears is different to what the audience hears.

Even after years of working with my singing teacher I still find it hard to believe when she tells me how I sound – but I know she's right. So, this is the "you" that other people recognise, but you don't.

Private – Our hopes and fears, our dreams and disasters, the things we don't like about ourselves, the things we're ashamed of or wish had never happened, the things we don't share with strangers – or maybe even those close to us. This is the place where those live. They're not all necessarily guilty secrets but they're things we're happier keeping to ourselves or a very select few.

Mystery/Potential – I always feel I'm going philosophical when I describe this window pane – all that "If a tree falls in a forest and no one is around to hear it, does it make a sound?" stuff (there's that technical term again). The problem here is you don't know if anything's in this area and nor does anyone else. It's a hypothetical place. But people discover talents, skills, strengths (both mental and physical) that they didn't know they had – sometimes during an emergency and sometimes by happy accident.

So, what's in your window panes? The model is always drawn in its starting state with four equal panes. But those panes change with learning and I believe there are two fundamental forces which are the basis of all personal and professional feedback.

These two forces reshape your window if you accept and engage with them. But this is entirely up to you. You can choose not to – it's safer that way. You won't look foolish or feel exposed – but you won't learn anything either.

When we conducted research into what organisations were looking for in their future leaders, the two most important characteristics were cultural adaptability and a proven willingness to learn. One of the best indicators of this was people who had travelled widely and exposed themselves to other cultures.

I've worked in 32 countries and that means that occasionally you find yourself not knowing what to do, or doing the wrong thing and looking stupid. I've been embarrassed many times, but I've learned at the same time too.

So, let's look at these two forces for learning

Feedback – Getting information from other people or your environment about what you've just said or done or how you appear to others. Feedback moves the vertical line in the window to the right – it shrinks the Blind Spots and increases the Public space.

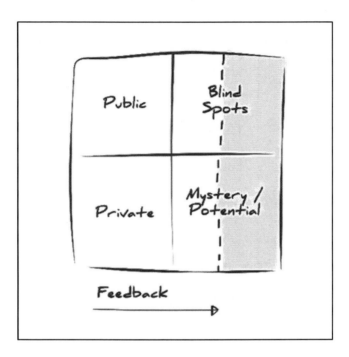

Most people know about feedback and indeed some have been exposed to it through 360 appraisals and the like.

Whatever the source, if you're willing to hear it and acknowledge it to be the truth (at least for other people) then you've got some more information about you that you didn't know before.

The lesser known or acknowledged second force is:

Disclosure – This is you sharing your thinking, your opinions, your views, your concerns, worries, doubts, weaknesses and indeed some of those hopes and fears. This moves the horizontal line downwards. This time the Private area is shrinking and there's a migration into the Public arena again so that grows even more.

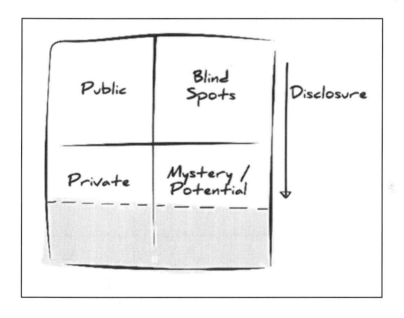

This is a bit trickier to think of as a source of learning for people because it's not inbound information. But the learning seems to come from the thinking, reflecting and realisations of just what's in that window pane or box, and the resulting relationship and intimacy that develops from releasing some of that.

OK, this part can seem rather intangible. But maybe, just maybe, by engaging with those forces and the learning that comes from them, something else happens: and that thing is the shrinking of the Mystery/Potential window pane.

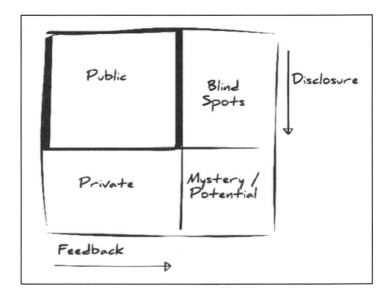

Perhaps you'll discover stuff about you that nobody realised – including you. Who knows?

More tangibly – and more directly to do with leadership – your Public window will have expanded and that's vital if you want people to buy into what you're all about and, indeed, recognise you as a leader or leading achiever. There's quite a bit of research that suggests people in leadership roles have more self-awareness that the average person (who is that "average" person, by the way? I've not met one yet).

More importantly, people expect leaders to have more of their public persona on display if they've chosen the limelight or spotlight. No use whining about your privacy if you want to be the person they follow.

So, this is the starting point for thinking about you in your leading achiever role. Until you have a way of thinking about who you are and acknowledging that the version of you may be different to other people, you can't begin that journey of personal and professional development and discovery.

The art of leading is the art of learning – and unless you make yourself available for learning with all the ups and downs that brings, then your window will stay the same. Then, sooner or later in this crazily unpredictable, wildly exciting and scary world we inhabit, you'll become an irrelevance and unable to make the difference you want to make. Here endeth the first lesson.

Actually, that's not true – those of you with an eye for detail will remember that I said there were two words that changed the first question and made all the difference. Those two words are "to them". So now the question is "Who do you think you are to them?" because what matters in leadership is what their expectations are of you and how well you meet or exceed their expectations.

Once you find this out you have a choice. You can accept that version of you as the role that's required, or choose to change their expectations. They might be surprised or disappointed, but authentic leadership is about being the real you and being true to yourself – not pretending to be what you're not.

In the next questions, I'll give you some more "stuff" which will clarify things even further or be a source of confusion. There's always the possibility that you delude yourself about being nice, or fair, or a team player or whatever.

I'd recommend a break now – whether it's a few minutes or a few days it doesn't matter. This approach works best if you go and do some thinking. For some of you that means asking others some questions and for some it's sitting in silence and doing some thinking and reflecting.

Worksheets

I've interspersed this book with worksheets and we've made these available online if you'd like to download them rather than write in the book: it's fine to do so, but I can never quite bring myself to write on the printed page (I think my mum's respect for books and authors has made a librarian of me).

The worksheets are there to help you collect your thoughts. If you want to use something else to record your thoughts, then great. But do, please, write something down. This is only the first question and things could change as we continue and there's a lot to carry around in your head.

Who do you think you are (to them)?

_____

- -

- -

- -

- -

- -

That's it – see you in Question Two.

The key to the ability to change is a changeless sense of who you are, what you are about and what you value

Stephen R. Covey

Question Two

What Do You Stand For?

It's quite hard to define exactly what our values are until they are challenged or called into question – either by other people's objections or we face a dilemma. We think we value total honesty and integrity but then our dying parent asks what the doctor said and we must decide whether to give them the painful truth or not. We may describe ourselves as a people person and a team player but realise that we only like being in teams when we're in charge and we're a people person when they just do what they're told.

Values affect our behaviour. In fact, they affect more than that, they affect the way we think and feel. They may also cause us to not even see or hear things which don't fit with our values and the way the world works as far as we're concerned. We filter out the inconvenient truths when it's too disturbing or just annoying to consider that things could be another way.

If you climb up a hill or a mountain and stand at the top on a clear day you can see for miles. The tourism signs call this a viewpoint. In our thinking lives we have a point of view – same thing. The way the world looks to us from that viewpoint is a unique perspective – and the way we think about the world from our hilltop is unique too.

You don't have to inhabit the planet for too long before you realise that, annoyingly, other people have hilltops too, and that their viewpoint is not the same as yours. They are, of course, the misguided ones. We may even consider them to have prejudices – but we don't, of course. We have strong views based on absolute fact.

I don't know where values come from, but I strongly suspect that they are nearly all the product of our upbringing. There is some evidence (I nearly said "stuff") that suggests there may be some genetic encoding that plays a part. I don't care. All I want to acknowledge is that we have values, we share some with a proportion of the population, and some values are significantly different to some others.

My personal experience is that it takes something pretty big to change our views and values. That's because life is a lot easier if things go the way we like them to go and there's a feeling of satisfaction and comfort from that. Most of us know the expression "comfort zone" and we live in that zone with our existing view of life, the universe and everything.

That "pretty big" something could be a significant traumatic event; it could be that the wealth of new evidence just becomes too big to ignore or we choose to buy into how a significant other in our lives sees the world.

One way of thinking about values (both our own and others') is to imagine that hilltop image I've been describing. You'll notice that there is some overlap with our first question **Who do you think you are?** – our values and how they play themselves out are, of course, part of who we are. Let's look at a hilltop, next:

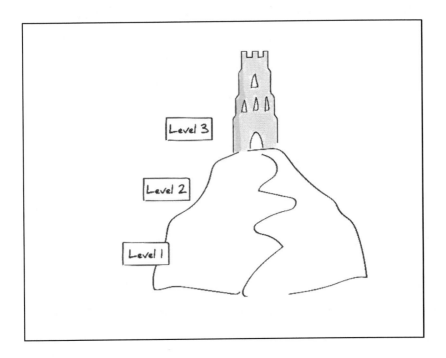

That's supposed to be Glastonbury Tor for those of you who are interested – and the very word "Glastonbury" could evoke some of your values and make you excited, fascinated or scornful of the people who gather for the music or those that are there for the spiritual forces.

Level 1 - the base of the hill on our map – is you in your simplest form. Who you are, what your name is, what you do, what hobbies you have or sports you play, where you live – all that stuff. If I only knew that much about you I wouldn't really know the whole person but, like the Johari window we talked about before, I could easily find out most of that because it's in the Public space.

Level 2 - Halfway up the hill. If I was to get to know you more (and was interested enough to ask) I could find out something about your thoughts and feelings. This is what a colleague of mine calls the "other than fact" level. It's your likes and dislikes, your thoughts about things, your opinions, your ideas. If you'd told me you played football I could ask you lots of questions about where, when, who with, etc. and stay at Level 1. If I asked you, "What do you get out of playing football?" or more simply, "Why do you like playing football?" I'd get a very different sort of answer. If I was a stranger, you might well feel uncomfortable because that's getting more personal.

We might never go any further than that in our relationship. If asked, we could say we were acquaintances – maybe even friends – but not share much more than Level 2.

This is probably where you get to at the networking breakfast – beyond the name badge and job title and vaguely into the realms of the person behind the badge.

Level 3 is the values level. We don't share this stuff with strangers unless we've voluntarily accepted this as part of the in-depth interview for a job. There's a trust issue here. This is where our vulnerability lies and if it's not a two-way sharing, then we'll feel we're being interrogated and invaded.

So Level 3 is where our values, motives, drivers, purpose, beliefs and truths reside. We're right up there on the hilltop now. Let's revisit that word "value" and think about what "valuable" means for a moment. We're now talking and thinking about what's important to us, what we value and hold to be valuable. So, the question now is not just, "Why do you play football?" but, "Why is playing football important for you?" or if you'd previously answered, "For the pleasure of winning," then, "Why is winning important to you?"

My mum (who had values about books as sacred objects) taught me that, at dinner parties, you don't discuss politics, religion or sex. Only later did I discover two things. Firstly, that dinner parties are much, much more interesting if you do and, secondly, that these are all Level 3 topics.

Also, that too much red wine hastens the journey to that hilltop which may then become the valley of remorse – but that's a whole other story.

So how do values affect your behaviour and consequently your operating style? Well, I think of it as a system with feedback loops. If you're able to behave in ways that fit with your values, then you feel good about yourself. That then feeds back and makes you keep doing it or doing more of it (whatever "it" is).

For example, if you are excited by winning, then you'll do whatever you can to make sure you win. If you do, you'll feel great and that will spur you on to train harder, play harder or find other ways to give you that winning buzz.

Your values and the resulting behaviour are what you're known for – they're a source of strength or an asset. If you were part of a negotiating team and you liked to win you'd be useful in driving for the best result.

Lots of energy, stamina, determination and that killer instinct that'll make sure we win at all costs…Uh-oh: killer instinct? Hmm, that's one of the problems with values – they're an asset until they're used inappropriately or in the wrong context, and then they're a liability.

When the negotiation needs to give up something for the good of the relationship that killer instinct value won't like it, and you'll probably be at least grumpy if not downright disruptive and destructive.

Now imagine that killer instinct in a leadership role – great when everybody is doing what they're told and the plan's working. What about when people need some support and a caring response? Can the winner do caring? Unlikely, actually – at least not in a sustained way. I've got a friend who is a cyclist and races to win – and she's very clear that it's not about taking part, it's about winning.

What do you think it's like going out for a ride with her? If you can't keep up – will she wait for you? Will she slow down and ride alongside you in a supportive way? Will she be OK with you slowing her down? Of course not; don't be silly.

So, when you list your values in the worksheet, have a think about what their flipside is – what happens if they're overdone. To give you a start I've suggested some value categories that might fit with how you see the world from your hilltop. I've written them as statements, so ask yourself if you could hear yourself saying this.

By the way, there's nothing inherently wrong with any values – including the killer instinct in the winner – but being aware of how it affects your behaviour, thinking, feeling and relationships is the key here.

I think life is about helping people who can't help themselves	
I think life's a competition and the one with the most medals/toys/accolades wins	
I think life should be about participating and being part of the team	
I think life is a fascinating problem to be logically solved	
I think life is about helping people to become self-sufficient and independent	
I think life is about campaigning and fighting for the underdog	
I think life is about developing strategies for winning by the rules	

Tick or mark the ones you think are like you (in your head, not on the page if my mum's watching) and then have a go at the worksheet.

My Values	Which means...	But if overdone...
Trust people to do the right thing	I respect people's motives and intentions	I can be gullible and get let down

Remember Johari? You could also ask others to say what they think your values are (feedback) and/or tell them what you think your values are (disclosure). There's lots of learning possibilities in there.

In the next question, we'll be thinking about you and your relationship to others. This leadership thing is not a solo occupation – even though some of you wish it was at times. See you in Question 3

Your decision to be, have and do something out of the ordinary entails facing difficulties that are out of the ordinary as well. Sometimes your greatest asset is simply your ability to stay with it longer than anyone else

Brian Tracy

Question Three

Why Should They Follow You?

The study of leadership has occupied scholars, academics and casual observers for nearly 200 years. Theories have bounced around and all, in their time, were certain they'd found the magic ingredient – the secret of leadership. The things you need, the pill you must swallow to be a leader. And not just a leader, a great leader. We're not thinking Alexander the Average here, are we?

Out of respect for all their hard work we should spend a few paragraphs looking at what they suggested, posited or downright insisted was the answer. You may like some or all of them and you may find some things useful – but I think you'll also get yourself tutting at some point and thinking "what nonsense is this?"

But remember, some of these ideas were around before cars, powered flight, microwaves, the internet and smartphones – so of course they sound old-fashioned.

Note your thoughts and what you like or loathe about some of the ideas here (sorry mum). It's great to disagree – just ask yourself <u>why</u> you disagree though, and stay curious. Getting too high on your hilltop stops you from listening, thinking and questioning.

So, our central question (the central question through history) was, "What makes a great leader?" This is roughly the historical order of the studies and emerging theories. This is not an exhaustive list – more to give you some food for thought. Get on with it then.

Theory	Like or Loathe	Why?
Great Man Theory Leaders are born not made. History has been shaped by a few great men. There may even be hereditary traits – look at ruling families. Darwinian laws of natural selection could apply – in the end only those with the innate qualities will lead		
Traits Theory There are qualities and aspects of personality which make some more fit for leadership than others. These character traits show themselves in leadership competencies. Officer selection in the armed forces and competency models in companies demonstrate and prove this		
Behavioural Theory Development of trait theory. Behaviours are what you do not what you think or feel. Things leaders say and do define the leadership agenda. *"Managers do things right – leaders do the right thing"*		
Situational Theory Refinement of behavioural theory. Leaders choose the right behaviours according to the situation or context. This depends on the performance readiness or ability of subordinates		

...And now for something completely different. Enter Mr Greenleaf and a whole new take on the subject. Such a new take that the macho corporate world mostly dismissed him as a religious irrelevance. This isn't real leadership surely? Hmmm, different hilltop.

His famous, ground-breaking essay was published in 1970 and here's the significant extract:

> *The servant-leader is servant first… It begins with the natural feeling that one wants to serve, to serve first. Then conscious choice brings one to aspire to lead. That person is sharply different from one who is leader first, perhaps because of the need to assuage an unusual power drive or to acquire material possessions…The leader-first and the servant-first are two extreme types. Between them there are shadings and blends that are part of the infinite variety of human nature.*

The Servant as Leader, Robert K Greenleaf, 1970

...And the notion of servant leadership was born. But – hang on a minute – isn't this strangely familiar? Hasn't it been around for millennia? Does the name Jesus, Buddha, Moses and a few others ring a bell? Yup – servant leadership was the model they were all ignoring. An inconvenient truth perhaps? Wrong hilltop? Anyway – bonkers. It'll never catch on.

Uh – hello? Probably the best-selling personal development book ever? *Seven Habits of Highly Effective People* by Stephen Covey...One of the biggest supporters of the notion of servant leadership.

> *Moral authority comes from following universal and timeless principles like honesty, integrity, treating people with respect.*
>
> **Stephen Covey**

For the record think about what you like/dislike about this one, too (that's what the blank box was for on the worksheet).

Theory	Like or Loathe	Why?
Servant Leadership The job of the leader is to serve the people. The best leaders are servant first. Rather than try to control, they create the environment of trust and respect which allows people to flourish		

…And there's more.

Even Greenleaf was arguably looking in the wrong place. It took Rob Goffee and Gareth Jones to shake things up in their article in Harvard Business Review article in 2001 by asking the right question…*Why Should Anyone Be Led by You?*

Note that this is no longer about what makes you a great leader, but about what makes them want to follow. You see, if they don't follow, you are not a leader – followers are the only thing that define leadership. Not qualities, traits, birth rights, background, charisma or anything else. If they don't follow, then you're not leading. You're walking to the Promised Land on your own - they're doing something more interesting. Some of our most iconic leaders have found themselves in this exact position.

One morning they woke up and they weren't the leader any more – Margaret Thatcher for example…And a few England football managers, too.

So, here's the worksheet for this question. Think of the camera and the interviewer's microphone pointed in your direction. It's live television and the question we'd like you to answer succinctly, honestly and from the heart (or hilltop) is.

Think about what you have to offer them, not what's good about you: and be ready for the interviewer's "So what?" follow-up question:

"I have 20 years' experience in software engineering"

"So what?"

Why should they follow you? What do you have to offer that makes them want to follow? In what way can you be of service to them?

I was going to stop there, but here's a bonus. At the centre of all this is the notion of trust. Unless they trust you they're not going to follow you, are they? Given that you're taking them somewhere they haven't been before, then this is a leap of faith on their part.

So, what builds trust and what reduces or destroys it? Charles H. Green's *Trust Equation* is a great way to think about you and your relationship with them. Here it is:

$$\frac{\text{Credibility} + \text{Reliability} + \text{Intimacy}}{\text{Self Orientation}}$$

The numerators (for the mathematically-minded amongst you) – the stuff above the line for the rest – are the factors that build or increase trust.

Credibility – Do people trust what you say? Is what you say founded in fact? Does what you say make sense to people? Is your story believable?

Reliability – Do you do what you say you are going to do? Do your actions match your words? Do you have a reputation for delivering?

Intimacy – Does it feel like this is the real you? Are you there as a person or a job title? Are they actually having a conversation with you?

The denominator is the thing that divides or reduces the equation (that's the bit below the line, guys – keep up).

Self-Orientation – Where's your focus: you or them? Are you doing this because it's good for you or others? How much is just about you?

Some people prefer to use the word Connection instead of Intimacy and some versions of the model talk of Self-Interest rather than Self-Orientation. Same model.

It's worth looking at some of the politicians in the public eye and noticing how this model works in your mind as you watch their performance – a great way to remind yourself what trustworthy and untrustworthy look and feel like.

This is leading us more and more into thinking about others more than you. For example, what's your relationship with, and impact on, other people.

So, the next question (**Question Four – What Will Be Different?**) is all about change as it affects other people. See you there.

If you want to make enemies, try to change something

Woodrow Wilson

Question Four

What Will Be Different?

I'm bored with the debate about the difference between leaders and managers for two reasons. One – the difference is really, really simple and doesn't need lengthy explorations, explanations and theses. Two – the managers always come off as second-best.

Let's sort this out fairly quickly. First of all, managers are not a lesser being than leaders. It's a different job, and the focus is in two different directions or tenses. Management is about what currently exists, what is there on the table and what needs control, stability, predictability. The word comes from the person who used to control the horses – and stems from the word for hand (main, mano, etc.).

Interestingly, menagerie is both "housekeeping" in French and a word for a collection of animals – reminds me of some teams I've had to manage in the past...

53

Leadership is about what doesn't exist – that all sounds a bit philosophical but what that means is it's in the future, it doesn't yet exist. A vision is not reality, it's a picture, indeed it's a dream (thank you, Martin Luther King Jr. for explaining that rather nicely). It's about moving to something different, changing what currently exists.

So, the difference is time. Management is about the present, Leadership is about the future. Tah-dah!

Ah – but the eagle-eyed amongst you will have noticed that I have quietly substituted "management" and "leadership" for "manager" and "leader". That's because, in today's real world, many people are doing both jobs. In fact, many of my coaching clients are doing three jobs: managing, leading and doing some of the actual work (great exercise on our programmes, by the way – draw a pie chart of how you spend your time now between leading, managing and doing, and how you'd like to spend it).

Sadly, managers do seem to get bad press. Not so much bad press as boring press. There are no books on charismatic management or visionary managers. We tend to associate magical powers with leadership and then quotes like, "Managers do things right; leaders do the right thing" take on a whole new mystical meaning. Messrs Bennis and Drucker are both credited with that particular one – and neither should be proud. That quote is a target of my scorn, by the way. It's nonsense. I've spent a lot of time working with managers who are cleaning up the mess left by the leader who did nothing like the right thing, but has now moved on to cause mayhem elsewhere.

OK, sermon over – now, where were we?

Ah, yes. Leadership is about the future and not the present. More importantly, leadership is about change, not maintenance. (see that word for hand in there?) So when we talk about managing change, we're talking about leading change. What we are managing is the reaction to the change at any given moment in time – more of that shortly.

William Bridges is another of my heroes. His work in the field of change has helped many of my client organisations to recognise what the leadership job is before, during and after change, and to recognise what goes on for people during any change process. To begin at the beginning, (to quote Dylan Thomas) Bridges noted that many leaders were incredibly poor at explaining where this change was going: what would exist, what the destination was; the "why and what" of the change. To quote from one of his articles on the topic:

> *"...until that vagueness can be cooked out of the undertaking and until the leaders of the change can not only explain it clearly, but do so in a statement lasting no longer than one minute, there is no way that they are going to be able to get other people to buy into the change."*

Leaders seem to go all mystical and magical when describing the future and so we hear words that at first seem inspiring – all brave new world, customer-centric, fully engaged and delightful – but that are hard to picture.

If you can't picture what someone is saying, then your brain must work harder and it's harder to buy into what they're proposing. Martin Luther King Jr. did not say, *"I have a hypothetical freedom concept which I want you to engage with"* – everyone can get what a dream is.

So, the description of what will be there when the change has happened must be as concrete, tangible and solid as possible. That's where our question comes from - **What will be different?**

Now, the other massively useful thing that William Bridges introduced to the world is transitions and how they are different to change. This is where the managing comes in.

Change is the thing itself, the process, the environment, the organisation, the brave new world, the promised land and the journey to get there. Transitions are the psychological processes of adaptation that people go through in relation to the change. Change is external to the person; transition is internal. If you move house or job or partner, that's a change – how you feel inside is the transition.

57

By the way, in those three examples of change I assumed it was voluntary, that it was your choice. Now imagine if it wasn't voluntary, that someone else had made that decision and you just had to live with it. Welcome to how people feel in relation to organisational change.

William Bridges wrote a whole book on Managing Transitions (that's the title by the way). I'll summarise some of this in a few paragraphs and we'll give you a worksheet to start illustrating what's happening with people you know, people who are responding and reacting to change.

A story has three phases. Beginning, Middle and End. Transition is the other way around. Endings, Middle, New Beginnings. For change to happen, something must end: something must be over or be about to be over. When the change has happened, people arrive at the beginning of a new chapter in their life.

Now notice that I said Endings, not Ending. That's because we're talking about people's reactions and responses to change and they're both very individual and could be several different things going on in response to one change.

Imagine receiving the news that, from next month there will be no more private offices (like yours) and you will now be working in an open-plan space with hot-desking. Just think of all the things that go through your head at this point.

Notice that there's bound to be more than one thought or feeling (hence the plural) and notice that it's all about what you're going to lose – this the Endings phase – characterised by feelings of loss. The focus and the conversation is all about what will be gone – privacy, status, structure, dignity, choice, peace and quiet – in the twinkling of a leader's vision for an office where everyone can communicate and interact.

Let's jump a few months' forwards in time. We're now in a place where the change has happened and people are now working in their allotted open space, having arrived early enough to get the desk they want that day and claimed their territory for the next few hours. This is the New Beginnings phase. It's characterised by people getting used to it, experimenting and finding out how to make it work for them. It's also characterised by not being the topic of conversation any longer; it's just the way we do things now. In the UK, not many people still mention ten shilling notes, half crowns and sixpences – but they did for quite a long time after we changed to decimal currency.

So, we've done the first and last phases of change and transition. What about that bit in the middle? William Bridges called this the Neutral Zone – it feels like nothing much is happening and it's a bit like a car in neutral; the engine's revving but the wheels aren't turning. I changed Bridges' model and coined the phrase Wilderness because that's what it feels like. You're wandering in the wilderness, you've left the old place behind, you haven't yet arrived and you feel disorientated, disengaged and pretty lonely. ("Where's everyone else?" "Am I the only one feeling this?")

It's not all bad news though – but it will feel like it right now. The Wilderness is also a place for rethinking, re-evaluation and asking yourself if this is really for you. Religious history has numerous examples of prophets and leaders taking to the wilderness to get clarity and make the big decisions. Unfortunately, this coincides with you feeling low on energy and motivation, so it's hard to step back and do that self-exploration and discovery.

Let's show this on a map.

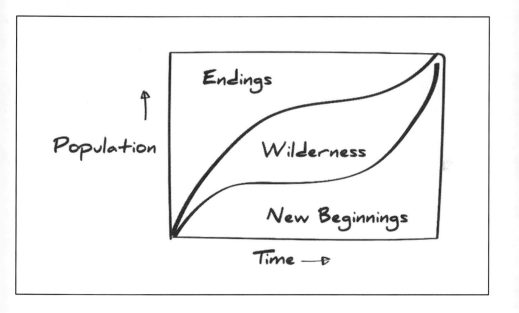

Imagine this is a population – a whole organisation or team or office, etc. At any moment in time people will be dotted all over the map. They won't all be in the same phase at the same time. Some will move quickly through Endings and the Wilderness to the New Beginning, whereas some will be in Endings weeks later – or perhaps permanently.

They may feel imprisoned by the change and the organisation – and resent every working and waking hour.

Bridges is very clear on this too – if they're never going to make it, they need to be helped out of the organisation as quickly and respectfully as possible. It's bad for their mental and physical health to remain, and it's not going to work for the organisation.

I have another way to describe it: "If you can't change the people; change the people".

So – worksheet time. Think of a change going on that you're part of. You may be the author or inventor of the change or it may be somebody else's idea. What phase of transition would you say people are at in relation to this change? What makes you say that? What do you need to do to help them move on? By the way, don't forget to include yourself on the map.

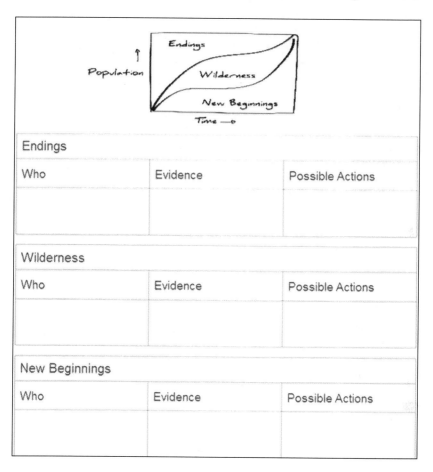

Given you can't do this alone and you need people's buy-in, the next question looks at where people are in relation to you and your ideas, proposals, vision or plans. See you on the other side: your side

The first method for estimating the intelligence of a ruler is to look at the men he has around him.

Niccolò Machiavelli, The Prince

Question Five

Who's On Your Side?

Let's start with three ways of talking about intelligence:

IQ – Intelligence Quotient

You know what IQ is – you wouldn't have got this far in the book (or life) without a certain level of Intelligent Quotient – thank you Alfred Binet and those who built on your original idea. Whether you love or loathe the IQ test itself as a measure of what intelligence is, most people accept the concept that cognitive scale gives some clue as to people's ability to function in business and life.

EQ – Emotional Intelligence

Peter Salovey and John D. Mayer used the term "Emotional Intelligence' in 1990, describing it as:

> *"a form of social intelligence that involves the ability to monitor one's own and others' feelings and emotions, to discriminate among them, and to use this information to guide one's thinking and action".*

Daniel Goleman, of course, went on to popularise the concept and many mistakenly think he's the inventor. Goleman argued that it was not cognitive intelligence that guaranteed business success but emotional intelligence. He described emotionally intelligent people as those with four characteristics:

- Good at understanding their own emotions (self-awareness)
- Good at managing their emotions (self-management)
- Empathetic to the emotional drives of other people (social awareness)
- Good at handling other people's emotions (social skills)

Six Questions for Leading Achievers

PQ – Political Intelligence

Not to be confused with Machiavellian intelligence which is almost entirely about obtaining power for self-gain at the expense of others. Mind you – I've always liked his quote about leading change:

> *"It ought to be remembered that there is nothing more difficult to take in hand, more perilous to conduct, or more uncertain in its success, than to take the lead in the introduction of a new order of things."*

Niccolò Machiavelli, The Prince

In my world, Political Intelligence (PQ) is the ability to understand how power works in a corporate entity and to be able to read the signs and manage the communications flow so that you build working relationships which help you achieve what you want to achieve. Still sounds Machiavellian I guess, but the intent is (I hope) because you're working for the common good, not just building your empire.

67

This question is very much focussed on Political Intelligence, but I think it's also built on a reasonable foundation of Emotional Intelligence. You won't be able to handle the inevitable setbacks, workarounds and diversions without some level of resilience and an ability to understand what other people want.

So, the first thing to acknowledge and accept is that you can't do this on your own. You need other people to engage with you, buy in to what you want to achieve, become supporters or sponsors of your cause and generally contribute to you getting more of what you want.

This isn't about forcing anyone to do anything or somehow hypnotising them with your magical gaze so that they are completely obedient and believe that resistance is futile.

This is about people wanting to work with you, seeing the benefits and buying in to what you're trying to achieve. Given what we talked about in the last question about leadership – this is about the future and change. You want them to join you on your journey.

This is a big topic and I'm going to focus on two aspects so that you start to do some thinking about it

1 Who's in your network?

2 How close is the relationship?

Who's in your network?

Networking as a thing you have to do has gained more and more column inches as the way business gets done today. Notice I didn't say "gained more popularity" because many people hate it – even though they know they should do it.

They grudgingly turn up at the dreaded networking breakfast and share what's usually a private part of their day with semi-strangers trying to slip a business card into their hand, all in the hope that a lifelong bond will be formed.

I think of networking as friendship with a purpose. I also created the name *Work Wide Web* ® as another way to describe your personal and professional network you need to survive and thrive in today's complex corporate world – whether you're in an organisation or you have to work with organisations.

Your *Work Wide Web* ® is the connected set of people you have a relationship with that might be useful to you at some point and that you are also willing to help.

This is probably one of the first mistakes people make – they assume the network is only there to serve them.

In fact, it's only sustainable if there's two-way traffic – an exchange of value. Reciprocation is the basic currency of successful networks.

There's a whole chapter to write on networking etiquette, skills, systems and the characteristics of successful networkers. I'll leave that to others but summarise what's needed with four things (bits of stuff) I keep in my head that serve me well

- *"Ask not what your network can do for you. Ask what you can do for your network".* (Sorry, John F. Kennedy)
- Nobody likes a hungry networker. Dig your well before you're thirsty.
- *"Seek first to understand then be understood"* (thank you, Stephen Covey)
- Remember the *Trust Equation*.

With these in mind let's set about mapping your personal and professional web of influence – the dynamic network of contacts and relationships that you need to build, maintain and develop to succeed.

Two things to consider then; their role and the closeness of the relationship:

Role – If networking is friendship with a purpose, what role do they play in your *Work Wide Web* ®? Forget, "they're just a friend" – their value to you is based on what they can do for you (and don't forget what you can do for them).

Informer – Keeps you up-to-date on what's going on. They're the ones that have heard about a new development or possible changes.

Adviser – More than just information, they're a wise head who can give you some helpful counsel and things to think about.

Connector – They know people and are willing to connect you with them as the need arises – they know who's got resources, information or knowledge.

Expert – Some people use the term "mentor". They are the key source of specialist knowledge in a particular field.

Sponsor – They have power and influence – inside or outside the organisation – they can mobilise important people to further your cause.

Promoter – They tell other people about you and what you do. News about you and your work is spread even while you're not in the room.

Your first job is just to produce a list of people you'd consider as being in your network. Just on a piece of paper for the moment, draw and label two columns: name and role.

If they play more than one role choose the main one. If you can't think what role they play – hmmm…You'll find the second phase of this exercise interesting.

OK, so there's your list. You may want to put it away for a time and come back to it again later. You'll have forgotten people or you may have rethought what someone's role is. By the way – this is not a social media "gather as many false friends as you can because more is better and makes you look good" exercise.

Six good contacts are a great starting point. Sixty network connections are hard work to maintain – and remember, this is meant to be a working network.

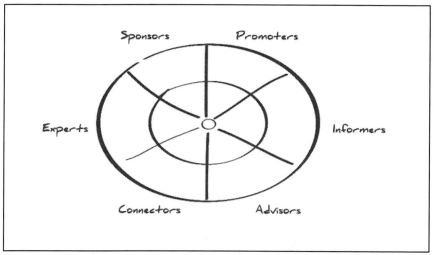

Once you feel you've got a good enough list to work with, you're going to put them on a map. That map looks like this before you start.

This is one instance where I think it's better to work outside the book – and probably on a larger piece of paper than A4 or Letter size. You're going to work in landscape (sideways) rather than portrait, too.

How close is the relationship?

So, you're going to place people on the map – just their initials perhaps in a bubble or circle. You've already decided their role - now you're going to be deciding how close the relationship is.

This is much more subjective, it's a felt thing. How well do you think you're connected with them? How much of a personal relationship is there? Those two things define closeness on this map.

This is a bit like the Intimacy/Connection factor we talked about in the *Trust Equation* (the stuff in this book isn't just thrown together at random, you know).

I'd recommend working in pencil or some people work with little sticky notes – and the techies draw it in PowerPoint or use mind-mapping software.

You're going to change your mind as you do it and the second phase of this exercise will be thinking about changes which, once implemented, change what's already on the map.

Anyway, once you've finished and your map is populated, it might look something like this.

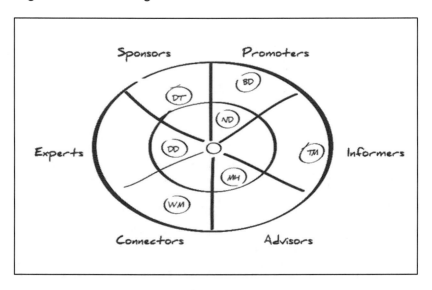

Now the thinking part and the big questions to consider.

- What roles are missing?
- Who needs to be closer?
- Who's wasting your time?

For your network to serve you well it needs to have the right people in it, performing the right roles, with the right level of connection or closeness.

Missing Roles - I'm not suggesting every role is equally important here but – given you don't know when you might need them and their contribution – it's useful to consider who could be in one of the missing roles.

Two of the common "missings" are Sponsors and Promoters. Of course, you can survive without them but you'll have to work harder, you'll reach a certain level of authority or connection where you're not known, and if you're not there nobody knows about you.

Closer – It's all very well having them on the map but if you hardly know them (and they you) then it's not really a relationship is it? If you phone them and they say, "who?" and you have to remind them where you met, then it's not very close is it? Be honest.

Just having their business card doesn't count. So, if you think they're going to be useful to you you'll need to do something about that.

Time-Wasters – Some of those dots on my map above are coded initials because I thought they'd be useful or they once were but now there's nothing of value there. Our worlds have moved on or I've realised that they're connected to me and only make contact when they want something.

BD is a classic case – he's been suggesting the possibility of new work ventures for more than three years now when he asks me for another outline for another possible programme that he's pitching to another possible client.

Last time I "forgot" to send him what he wanted…He probably found someone else.

Update – He just phoned (I am not kidding – I thought it was spooky too) and left a message saying there are some opportunities that I might be able to help with…I am not booking a holiday in the Bahamas on the strength of the call.

Could this be the occasion when he actually comes up with the goods? I sent him an email with a 15% hike on my current rates and told him to let me know…nothing back so far.

I'm mostly a nice person – but nice is not the key to making your network a productive, sustainable source of mutually-beneficial opportunities. Nice gets you wasting time and energy being well… nice.

Meanwhile I had a great lunch with WM and realised that he's more of an adviser than a connector now. I hadn't seen him for a year and both our lives have changed somewhat. Closeness on the map was and is in the right place – role was wrong.

By the way there's no such thing as a free lunch. I paid because I felt it was worth it – I wasn't just being nice.

So, the second phase (and a regular housekeeping task – remember "menagerie" earlier in the book?) is to rethink and reorganise your collection of people. I've got a worksheet for you.

You're going to be thinking about three factors that need to be increased or decreased:

- **Contact** – How frequently are you in touch with them? When was the last time you spoke to them or had an email exchange? How much more (or less!) contact do you now want?
- **Closeness** – Who on the map do you need to be closer or to move to the outer circle (less time spent dealing with them)?
- **Contribution** – What role do you need from them (this could be a change of role) and what do you do for them? This is about reciprocation so if you're not useful to them in some way, then this isn't going to last.

With these factors in mind you can start updating your map – and make it a habit.

People on our programmes have often found this particular exercise one of the most illuminating and it has changed their world of work. They recognise that they have to move their focus from working in the role or business, to working on their role within it. Building their connections, reputation and relationships and digging their well before they're thirsty.

	Who	
	More (+)	Less (-)
Contact How often do you need to be connecting with them?		
Closeness What distance do you want between you and them?		
Contribution What do you need from them and what can you offer them?		

This is about increasing your presence – and that's a very big bit of what we're going to talk about in our sixth and final question... (good link, Clive.)

People have forgotten how to tell a story. Stories don't have a middle or an end any more. They usually have a beginning that never stops beginning

Steven Spielberg

Question Six

Who Listens When You Speak?

Leadership is a stand-out role – that means you are distinctive, you are noticed, and (going way back to Johari Window) your Public area is bigger than the average person. They want to know what you're thinking and what your thinking is all about. They want to understand what it is you're trying to get them to buy in to and trying to understand why they should follow you.

The challenge is how to get all of that stuff into a package that engages them, interests them – even excites them – and gives them all they need to make their choice. However, you haven't got much time. I don't mean you're busy (but of course you are) – I mean you haven't got much time before they lose interest or find something else more attractive.

Without them you will just be a "voice calling in the wilderness," to quote Matthew, 3:3.

Scarily, their attention span (notice how it's always 'them', not me or you) is getting shorter. A recent study showed the average human attention span has fallen from the 12 seconds reported in 2000, (around the time the mobile revolution began) to 8 seconds. Goldfish, meanwhile, are believed to have an attention span of 9 seconds.

Now this issue isn't new but it is more extreme. Speechwriters and speechmakers have, for centuries, been trying to get people's attention and buy-in. They didn't have PowerPoint to help them – they used the spoken word.

Martin Luther King Jr. didn't have PowerPoint during the March on Washington for Jobs and Freedom on August 28, 1963; he used his mastery of the spoken and written word to engage, inspire and align 250,000 people from the steps of the Lincoln Memorial in Washington, D.C.

What they all used is the power of rhetoric -the art of effective or persuasive speaking or writing. Funny word – and its spelling gives you a clue how long it's been around. Aristotle was big on rhetoric – he described three modes of persuasion - logos, pathos, and ethos. Appealing to a sense of logic, appealing to emotion and demonstrating your credibility and character (ethos is Greek for character).

Right – enough history. Let's talk about what's between their ears. Everyone's got a brain. In its very simplest terms you've got to get your message in there and to have it stay there long enough for them to register their interest. You talk at about 150 words per minute and you've got 8 seconds.

That means your first 20 words had better hit the target – or targets, since we've got two areas of the brain we want to focus on – the logical bit and the emotional bit. See how technical this is?

Let's increase my credibility with you by mentioning some names for parts of the brain – we want to focus on the prefrontal cortex (the logical bit) and the limbic system (the emotional bit).

We've got to make it through the prefrontal cortex with the least resistance and get lodged in the limbic system to create some emotional connection. Rhetoric plays a part in this but it's not the only device. You need to make your messages brain-friendly – and that means working with, rather than against, the way the human brain receives and processes information.

Four things (including rhetoric) help your message get there and stay there.

- **Structure** - The brain likes things in an order that's quick and easy to understand – ABC, 123, XYZ for example
- **Connection** – To help efficient storage and recall, the brain makes connections with existing information and knowledge. You can help by linking your new stuff to their existing stuff.
- **Imagery** – We think and remember in pictures most of the time. You can remember your favourite holiday or your loved ones' faces instantly.
- **Rhetoric** – There are verbal and written devices and structures which help people remember – they're what speechwriters and copywriters use all the time – you know what the Nike slogan is, don't you?

Now I've just done something there which is important – I've told you what I'm going to tell you. That's structure in action. Your brain is now a little more prepared for what's coming – and hopefully I've included enough to pique your interest by connecting to things you already know.

Let's go into more detail. I'll use Martin Luther King Jr.'s "I Have a Dream" speech quite a lot because it is simply a masterpiece. I'm not suggesting this is how you do it (your audience may be a little smaller) but notice what it looks like when performed with such mastery. I'm probably going to start referring to him as MLK because it takes up less space.

Structure – There's a great structure that's been around for millennia and is used in films, stories, speeches, books, plays, television programmes, news bulletins and music: Beginning, Middle and End. It's a source of constant confusion to me that this brilliantly simple form gets forgotten as soon as PowerPoint comes along.

I've witnessed many hundreds of Middle-Middle-Middle presentations with, "Uh, any questions?" as the stunning finale.

There's a very clear start to the "I Have a Dream" speech – where MLK connects with his audience and outlines where he's going:

> *"Let us not wallow in the valley of despair. I say to you today my friends -- so even though we face the difficulties of today and tomorrow, I still have a dream. It is a dream deeply rooted in the American dream."*

And the ending is very clear

> *"Free at last! Free at last! Thank God Almighty, we are free at last!"*

Connection – There's two bits to this. Connection to what they already know and connection between the bits you're telling them about. When you watch the news, you pay more attention to the items that are close to home or close to a topic you're interested in.

In speeches and presentations, you make that connection explicit. You find the thing that they connect with. What they're interested in, what their role is, what they associate with.

"Some of you have come from areas where your quest for freedom left you battered by storms of persecution and staggered by the winds of police brutality"

said MLK. Within the speech, of course, his "I have a dream" repetitions worked to connect all the pieces.

Fascinatingly this dream theme wasn't in the plan, it was only when Mahalia Jackson shouted, "Tell them about the dream Martin…" that he went down the now iconic route.

The main theme was the Liberty Bell and the notion of freedom. Towards the end he starts to use "Let Freedom Ring" as the connecting phrase.

Imagery – With no PowerPoint, no video and just his voice, MLK had to create pictures in people's minds. He uses word pictures of America – "hilltops of New Hampshire", "mighty mountains of New York", "the snow-capped Rockies of Colorado", "the curvaceous slopes of California". You may not have visited any of these places but you can picture them from what he says.

The message is clear. Use words and phrases that people's brains can use to form pictures. You can't picture an "imagined freedom concept", but you can picture a dream.

Brilliant. I have read and analysed that speech repeatedly as part of my work and every time I find something else to marvel at – and, most importantly, be moved by.

Rhetoric - On top of everything else it's a masterpiece example of the use of rhetorical devices. Let me just illustrate two or three that you can use:

Contrasting Pairs – "To be or not to be", "not this but that", "not there but here", "not if but when", "black and white", "young and old", "past and present", "give and take" are all contrasting pairs.

There's something about them that helps us to picture the difference – and helps us engage and identify with the message.

One of my favourites from MLK's speech is:

> *"…I have a dream that my four little children will one day live in a nation where they will not be judged by the color of their skin but by the content of their character"*

Three Part Lists – In truth, we don't know why or how but the number three seems to be particularly persuasive and gives a sense of completeness. Speechwriters and copywriters use it extensively.

Putting things in threes, whether it be three-word slogans or lists of three items is magical. If you've got things to tell people, limit the list to three where possible and make the third one the most important. "Red White and Blue", "Liberté, Egalité, Fraternité" "Faith, Hope and Charity", "Eat' Love, Pray", "Earth, Wind and Fire", "Blood, Sweat and Tears", "Just Do It", "Yes We Can" – you get the idea. If you're clever you combine contrasting pairs and three part lists:

> *"…little black boys and black girls will be able to join hands with little white boys and white girls as sisters and brothers"*

And if you've only got one thing to say, say it three times:

> *"Free at last! Free at last! Thank God Almighty, we are free at last!"*

Repetition – A simple device but sadly missing in so many presentations I see and hear. Technically there's the anaphora (repetition of a word or phrase at the beginning of successive clauses) which is what MLK was using with "I have a dream" repeated nine times, and "Let freedom ring" repeated ten times.

That's a very orator speech-y thing – less likely to be used by you in presentations and reports. But remember that structure we started with? Like the TV news, if you repeat your main items three times you're helping cement those things in the receiving brain.

So, your worksheet exercise is to go back to Question Three – "Why Should They Follow You?" and see if you can write a 50-word piece which captures what you have to offer.

It should have a Beginning, Middle and End, make a connection with their interests, use language that creates pictures and contain at least one of the rhetorical devices.

Why should they follow you?

50 words with a Beginning, Middle and End

Summary

See that? You know what's coming now. You know I'm coming to the end and I'm going to repeat some of the main things I want you to remember.

- In a leadership role people need to know your thinking and engage with it if they're going to buy-in to your ideas.
- Attention span is getting shorter and you need to capture their attention in your first 20 words.
- Make your message brain friendly by using Structure, Connection and Imagery.
- Use rhetorical devices like Contrasting Pairs, Three Part Lists and Repetition.
- And if you only take one thing from this, remember Beginning, Middle and End.

Now this is not the end. It is not even the beginning of the end. But it is, perhaps, the end of the beginning.

Winston Churchill

And now, the end is near…

I couldn't use Summary again and I don't have much more to say. I hope that you'll want to explore even further and join me on one of our programmes. I'd love to work with you if you want to learn and accept the personal challenge of exploring, experimenting and discovering.

Below are some of the quotes and words of wisdom that have shaped my thinking and approach to personal and professional development and the design of the "Six Questions for Leading Achievers" programme:

"Judge a man by his questions rather than by his answers"

Voltaire

"If you think you understand a problem, make sure you are not deceiving yourself"

Albert Einstein

"The problem is not to find even cleverer people to come up with the answers, but to find people to ask good questions"

Reg Revans

"In a world of change, the learners shall inherit the earth, while the learned shall find themselves perfectly suited for a world that no longer exists."

Eric Hoffer

"To have seen a dozen Nobel Laureates helping each other to ask totally fresh questions explained what action learning is"

Reg Revans

"We cannot solve our problems with the same thinking we used when we created them"

Albert Einstein

"We do not need, and indeed never will have, all the answers before we act. It is often through taking action that we can discover some of them."

Charlotte Bunch

"Don't let your learning lead to knowledge. Let your learning lead to action"

Jim Rhon

"I have never met a man so ignorant that I couldn't learn something from him"

Galileo Galilei

"The top experts in the world are ardent students. The day you stop learning, you're definitely not an expert"

Brendon Burchard

"Throw yourself into life as someone who makes a difference, accepting that you may not understand how or why"

Benjamin Zander

"When you make a mistake, throw your hands in the air and say "How fascinating!""

Benjamin Zander

"In the book of life, the answers are not in the back"

Charlie Brown in Peanuts

"But the worksheets are on the web…"

Clive Hook

The Six Questions Worksheets

If you would prefer to not upset my mother by writing in this book – oh please don't tell me you already have – you can download copies of the worksheets from our web site. We'll need a name and email address from you so that we know who's looking at our stuff and hopefully benefitting from the insights and learning. You'll find them at www.clearworth.com/6QLAWorksheets

Thank you for your interest and your commitment to learning. I'd love to work with you again so please keep in touch and we'll keep you up-to-date with things we've developed or new approaches we're taking.

Clive Hook

Programme Director

ClearWorth

#0187 - 230117 - C0 - 210/148/5 - PB - DID1730111